TIM
OMOTOSO

PRAYER BONANZA

First published in paperback - July, 2011

© Tim Omotoso 2011

Published by Tim Omotoso

info@timomotoso.org | www.timomotoso.org

British Library Cataloguing-in-data

A catalogue record for this book is available from the British Library.

PREFACE

This prayer book is divinely inspired to make you 'a prayer addict'. Prayer along with the Word of God is your lifeline to the Creator and it enables you to shape your world. **Prayer Bonanza** is a perfect tool in your hand that will push you out of prayerlessness and enhance your intimacy with God. The principles outlined in this book are designed to challenge you as a reader to 'become prayer itself' as *"men ought always to pray and not to faint,"* (Luke 18:1).

Each prayer points are real life experiences (Luke 22:44) and contain a revelation about the mysteries of God and the operations of the spiritual realm. Whether you are seasoned in prayer or struggling to communicate with the heavens, Prayer Bonanza will enable a healthy dialogue to develop between the natural (you), and the supernatural (the Creator). You will understand the requirements of answered prayer and receive the right vision for your life.

As you read and apply the prayer points, remember to season them with songs of thanksgiving and praise unto God. Choose the manner of your position in prayer, but no repetition should be entertained. When your prayer life is intact you will contact the heavenlies and grab your eternal grapes. Always remember that your life is fragile and you need to handle it with prayer.

Tim Omotoso

TIM OMOTOSO

PRAYER BONANZA
- PART 1 -

(An extract of a message preached by Tim Omotoso at a camp meeting in Pietermaritzburg, South Africa, on 3rd June 2001.)

"And Jabez was more honourable than his brethren: and his mother called his name Jabez, saying, because I bare him with sorrow." 1 *Chronicles* 4:9

A lot of people are honourable, but their names are not. If the name given to you by your family is not honourable, Jabez showed us what to do. The Bible says, *"And Jabez was more honourable than his brethren: and his mother called his name Jabez, saying Because I bare him with sorrow."* Because his mum was in sorrow, she decided that the child born at that time must also share of her sorrow; she did not know the implication of the name. Jabez was honourable but his name was dishonoured.

"And Jabez called on the God of Israel ...." When trouble calls on you, call on God; call on the God of Israel. He did not go to his mum and say, you are in charge of my sorrow, you are the one that caused this thing to come into my life. Remember you are not fighting against flesh and blood. The reason why we do not win battles is that we try to fight battles that are not ours to fight.

So Jabez called on the God Israel, and I want you to see what Israel means: NATION. He could have called on the God of Jacob, because God never said that I am God of Abraham, God of Isaac and God of **Israel** (Exodus 3:6). He did not call it that way at that level. He called the God of Israel apart from the God of Jacob. But do not forget that Israel means Jacob: it is an extension of a name, and a conversion of identity.

Jacob himself was another person altogether who showed to the world that God is a God of mercy and that He does not require sacrifice from man before you can be loved of Him. For this reason, Jabez called on the God of Israel; he needed multiplication in his life. That is why he did not call on the God of Jacob, but of Israel. That is the power working in Him.

What is power? Power is something that intensifies an effort beyond ordinary level. Power is something that is activated when you are in your weakest position. It actually catapults you to a realm beyond ordinary. You have power here, for instance, when you say, 'I shall receive power', as you read in the Bible: *"But ye shall receive power after that the Holy Ghost is come upon you........."* What it means is this: this is your life, for example, (a keyboard that I have switched off). Look! I am pressing it very hard (keys on the keyboard). This is how you have been struggling in your life all this while. The Lord wants to play you like a musical instrument in his hand, but without power – no sound!

The power concept is not merely a necessity but a compulsion. It is not something you are to think about, you do not need a second thought about it, it is now or never. Some people live their lives as if they are walking corpses. You can actually live when you are 70, with God's power and look as if you are just 20 years old. POWER RENEWS.

So, look at this (keyboard); I want to play the song "How great thou art" (The man of God presses the keys of the keyboard whilst the power is off), am I not deceiving myself?

This is how many believers have been deceiving themselves. They have been playing the keyboard of their life in the absence of power. Power enables you to activate your activity. Jabez went to a man who had power over living and non-living things. He cried to the God of Israel and there are five things he said in his prayer, and these are worth emulating. Now, before you read on, confess your sins and ask for forgiveness - then read on and meditate on every prayer point. Brethren, **"meditation is medication"**.

PRAYER ONE

There are five prayer points there, because we have five sense organs. And Jabez is five letters. Thank God for this. And Jabez called on the God of Israel. God means Grace Or Disgrace. Grace or disgrace is GOD, whichever side you take God, He will be to you. God knows how to disgrace and knows how to grace people. That is the full meaning of G-O-D.

Now, he said in the first statement, *"Oh that thou wouldest bless me indeed."* Most people do not understand the concept of blessing. Open the Bible to 3 John 1:2. *"Beloved, I wish above all things that thou mayest prosper ..."* The first prayer Jabez prayed was one of blessing. You have to prosper first. I want you to understand this matter of prosperity and its concept. I want you to liken your life to this keyboard. You have been like this keyboard - silent: your life has been silent; nobody knew you were around because you have never made an impact. Read again, *"Beloved, I wish above all things that thou mayest prosper and be in health, even as thy soul prospereth."* It's God's wish that you prosper, but God's wish must be your own wish. Your own personal ambition is inferior to divine direction.

Your level of prosperity is going to be determined by your thinking faculty in line with biblical injunction. Prosperity has no limit before God. If you want God to live with you in a gutter it is prosperity. For God was with Joseph even in the prison, it's prosperity, because God was with him. But, God was with him in the pit, not for him – God may be with someone without being for him/her.

Jabez was honourable and he was okay, but being okay is not the standard that God wants for your life. Because above all things, God wants you to prosper according to how your soul prospers. Your soul is the thinking faculty. For instance, you want to buy a car, and the level of prosperity in your soul/mind, is Volkswagen. God will give you a Volkswagen, because that is how your soul prospers. However, that does not mean that is the end of prosperity, but rather that your soul desires what God gives. God gave you your soul's desire. So, the level of prosperity begins from your thinking faculty, "*as your soul prospereth*".

If you have it in your soul that you must not die in a one-bedroom flat, the moment you say, "God, I want an enlargement of coast," God will ask you in your brain, what exactly you want? Every time people came to Jesus for healing, even blind people, he will ask them, "What can I do for you?" He knew straight away that they needed healing, but He would never force healing in their lives. Perhaps they had something better than healing in their souls.

Otherwise, God will not give allowance for men to ask, because God knows He has planted something on the inside of you that could think for God, on your behalf. I'm not going to tell God to just take me to Heaven, I'm going to tell God to take me to Heaven and give me a whole nation in Heaven, not just a room.

Your soul has to prosper first before your life can prosper. If your soul is not prosperous your life can never be prosperous. If you have a poor man's mentality, you're going to live like a poor man. That is the reason why, when you pray, the Bible says, we have to renew our mind. The Bible wants you to prosper. He has interest in the prosperity of His servants. Psalm 35:27 *"let them shout for joy, and be glad that favour my righteous cause: yea, let them say continually, let the Lord be magnified, which hath pleasure in the prosperity of His servant."* I want you to understand, God is interested. He has pleasure."

Why should you depend on the mentality of people who tell you that if you prosper you are going to hell?

After power, then riches and then wisdom. You can never have wisdom without riches. The power of God will propel you into proper propelling, so that you can have things that have been designed for you. Every day there must be increase in your life; there must be an enlargement of coast. Life must not be stagnant – man was not made for stagnation. Your life must be on the move. **A Chronic problem requires a chronic solution.**

And Jabez said *"that thou wouldest bless me indeed"*. Bless me is not enough; God has to bless you, but how? INDEED. Anything you do without the language indeed is not acceptable in the heavenlies. "If the son shall set you free you shall be free indeed."

-out the language indeed is not acceptable in the heavenlies. "If the son therefore shall make you free ye shall be free indeed."(John 8:36)

PRAYER TWO

"*... and enlarge my coast*," is an extension. God is going to bless me indeed but that's not enough. Also, do what? Enlarge my coast. God can bless a man indeed without enlarging his coast. Some people have money but they don't know how to spend it. They won't remember the poor and they don't remember the widows (read Mt 25:35). Pray now, and say, "Lord, enlarge my coast."

PRAYER THREE

"*... And that thine hand might be with me*," - that means after blessing me indeed, enlarging my coast, let your hand be upon me, so that all these things will not waste away. Don't let enemies come and take them away. Let your hand be upon me so that wherever I go your hand goes with me. **Poverty does not make you holy, it compounds unholy living.**

The Lord stripped the devil naked in Heaven and cast him to the Earth to become poor. Angels are in Heaven because they are in prosperity. Who is poor? Devil and demons, because they are devils. Are they not wicked? They are, because they have no prosperity from above. They only came to steal, to kill, to destroy. The devil has no house on Earth; he is an illegal immigrant. It was also said in the book of Job, "I go to and fro the Earth." Pray now on this point.

PRAYER FOUR

"And thou wouldest keep me from evil" - when God blesses a man, there are evil doers who are looking for the blessing to steal. Pray for sustenance and security from evil doers.

PRAYER FIVE

"That it may not grieve me" - another version says, *"that I may be free from pain"*. That means, give me good health. Brethren, "health is wealth". This prayer means, Lord, when you give me good money and good prosperity, give me good kidney to drink good drink. When you give me a good liver don't let me be grieved. If I have a hole in my heart, fill it for me, so that I can have long life in you.

There is a mark in my Bible – an exclamation mark "!" after the fifth prayer – a sign, "a ha", which means, all these cannot be done by men. And after that, God came in, because there is a mark standing between God and the five prayers. Which means I rest my case in God's hands. If you ask for bread God will not give you a stone, and if you ask for fish He will not give a snake.

"and God granted him that which he requested" - in the same manner, He will grant you that which you have requested, if you pray likewise. Remember, God granted him based on his prayer points; and not according to his name, Jabez. God will bless you too in Jesus' name. Amen.

<u>SCRIPTURE READING:</u> *Psalm 103: 1 - End*

Memory Verse: *"Hear my prayer, O God; give ear to the words of my mouth." Psalm 54:2*

PRAYER POINTS:

1. God, make me a whole human being and restore anything lacking in my life, in Jesus' name.

2. God give me my lost glories, charisma and wisdom.

3. God, I want to see your face; I want you to make an everlast -ing covenant with me and write my name in the book of life unconditionally, in Jesus' mighty name.

4. God, remove the sin which grew with me from my mother's womb. Destroy every negative background that I have. Deal with me and my background, create in me a clean heart and renew a right spirit within me.

5. Father, in the name of JESUS CHRIST, the son of David, come today and destroy the covenant my parents had, the first day they met together which is now bringing/creating problems in my life.

6. **Call the name of Jesus three times** –Then say, Lord, destroy any spirit of discord, envy, hatred and jealousy that is in me.

7. Let the spirit of Christ dwell in me in all wisdom and power.

8. Thank you Lord for all the answered prayers.

SCRIPTURE READING: *Isaiah: 54:1-End*

Memory Verse: *"For I know the thoughts that I think toward you, saith the LORD, thoughts of peace, and not of evil, to give you an expected end." Jeremiah 29:11*

PRAYER POINTS:

CALL THE NAME OF JESUS THREE TIMES, HIS BLOOD THREE TIMES.

1.   Lord, cancel every negative word I have spoken against my -self.

2.   God, restore unto me the glory of the cross of Calvary so that my life can be meaningful.

3.   Lord, I need new eyes: so that I might be able to discern and distinguish between friends and enemies, in Jesus' mighty name.

4.   Install in my life the engine of prayer, in Jesus name.

5.   God, anoint me mightily against my enemies, over living and non-living things.

6.   Father, make me a pillar in everything that I do, in Jesus' name.

7.   Lord, destroy everything the enemies have given me to de -stroy, to monitor or to trouble my life, in Jesus' name.
      (a)   Lord, return unto me all my goodness, successes, pros -perity, that I lost in transit.

(b)   Destroy the breast covenant and any other covenant made against me in Jesus' name.

(c)   Destroy every covenant I made with death and the graveyard through imaginations and dreams.

8.   Lord, destroy all the people hired to destroy my life and to monitor all my movements. Destroy them Lord, in Jesus' name.

9.   Lord, my enemies have stripped me naked; please clothe me with your garment of righteousness.

10.   Thank you Lord for all the answered prayers.

SCRIPTURE READING: *Luke 17:11-19, Ps. 91:1-end*

Memory Verse: "The silver is mine, and the gold is mine, saith the LORD of hosts." Haggai 2:8

PRAYER POINTS:

CALL THE NAME OF JESUS THREE TIMES, HIS BLOOD, THREE TIMES.

1. Lord, I confess my sins of pride and arrogance; please forgive me. I drive away the spirit of pride and arrogance from my life to where it came from, in Jesus' name.

2. God, I implore you to give me your divine favour, destroy all my destroyers. Let no demon/devil/witch or wizard steal or corrupt my divine favour, in Jesus' name.

3. Give me the power and the engine of prayer.

4. Lord, give me power over persons, places or things and over living and non-living things, in Jesus' name.

5. Lord, destroy every eye monitoring my life and all the people hired to follow me wherever I go.

6. God, come and immunise my spirit (spiritual injection). Im -munise my soul and body against every hurt; against all my enemies and all their arrows and weapons, in Jesus' mighty name.

7. Lord, destroy every power holding back my success, and breakthrough. Destroy every snail spirit and any spirit of

delay tactics in my life. Lord, bind every power operating and militating against my life, in Jesus' name.

8. Lord, return unto me the glory of my life sevenfold: the glory taken away by my tongue, my parents, my friends and my enemies.

9. Thank you for all the answered prayers.

SCRIPTURE READING: *Isaiah 43:1 - end*

Memory Verse: *"But those mine enemies, which would not that I should reign over them, bring hither, and slay them before me." Luke 19:27*

PRAYER POINTS:

1. Lord, bring here enemies of mine that do not want me to reign over them, and slay them before me, in Jesus' name.

2. Give me a gift that has not been given to any man before, and destroy in me every shadow-chasing project, in Jesus' name.

3. Lord, you are the only one who knew me from my youth. You were the only one there when I was formed in the secret of my mother's womb; you alone knew me before I came into existence; therefore why should the enemies have dominion over my life? Lord, whence comes this darkness, this failure, this nakedness? Return unto me all my blessing, my success and my breakthrough taken away by the dogs of this world - by monkeys, by cats, by fishes, by enemies in the sea. In Africa, America, Europe, Asia, the Antarctic, Pacific, Indian, Atlantic oceans; in the firmament, under the ground, on top of mountains etc. By living or non-living things.

4. Lord, destroy all the trees and seeds the enemies planted in me before and after I was born.

5. Destroy all the agents of darkness that have no place to live except in my body. Remind them that they have lost their abode and that my body is the house of God/the temple of the HOLY SPIRIT. Therefore they have no right to stay in my

body. Drive them out! Every sickness and infirmity either known or unknown should go, in JESUS' NAME! All the slip -pery hands should depart from my life, in the mighty name of Jesus.

6.   Lord, remove all of the negative 'BUTs' in my life.

7.   Thank you Lord for all answered prayers.

<u>SCRIPTURE READING</u>: *Ezekiel 37: 1-14*

Memory Verse: "Ask, and it shall be given you; seek and ye shall find, knock, and it shall be opened unto you." Matthew 7:7

PRAYER POINTS:

CALL THE NAME OF JESUS THREE TIMES, HIS BLOOD THREE TIMES.

1.   Let your kingdom come to my life, rule and have your way in my entirety, in Jesus' name.

2.   Father, resurrect all my dead projects, in Jesus' mighty name.

3.   Lord, send your thunder and lightning to anything or anyone waging war against me, in Jesus' name.

4.   God, send oppressing angels upon whosoever or whatsoever is holding my blessing, in the mighty name of Jesus.

5.   Lord, destroy every spirit that makes me lose my memory, in the mighty name of Jesus.

6.   O Lord, set on fire anyone in charge of my life, in Jesus' name.

7.   God, remove any mark of slavery and failure that is on me, in Jesus' name.

8.   Lord, separate me from people with a mark of slavery and failure, in the mighty name of Jesus.

9.   Lord, come today and resurrect my life, let all my dry bones

arise and live, let flesh cover my dry bones, in Jesus' mighty name.

10. Thank you Lord for all answered prayer.

SCRIPTURE READING: *Joel 2:28-29, Acts 2:1-4*

Memory Verse: "God is a Spirit: and they that worship him must worship him in spirit and in truth." John 4:24

PRAYER POINTS:

1. Lord, I want to worship you in spirit and in truth. Give me a new heart of love, joy and peace. Fill my heart with your presence.

2. Lord, teach me the Bible, educate me in the scripture and em power me in your words, in Jesus' name.

3. Lord, change my negative character that has its origin in my family, and all addictions that might destroy me, in Jesus' name.

4. Lord, all demons assigned to me waiting till I get to the top, I cast them out, in Jesus' mighty name.

5. God, I want to raise a standard with you than all my contem -poraries and friends. I want to be unique. Use every power in Heaven and Earth to raise me up.

6. Lord, don't give me the Earth and the fullness alone, but give me yourself for greater exploits, in Jesus' name.

7. Lord, give me the engine of prayer. Give me an ability to pray continuously. Lord, install in me your engine of prayer. Engine of prayer come into me, in Jesus' name.

8. Thank you Lord for all answered prayers.

SCRIPTURE READING: Matthew 28: 18

Memory Verse: *"Now unto him that is able to do exceeding abundantly above all that we ask or think, according to the power that worketh in us." Ephesians 3:20*

PRAYER POINTS:

1.   Lord, any part of my body that has surrendered to the Philis
      -tines whilst I was asleep, bring it back and set me free in Je
      sus' name. (Samson had two parts of his body surrendered to
      the Philistines, his eyes – wisdom, and his hair – power).

2.   Lord, give me power over everything such as wind, fire, wa
      -ter, moon, stars, sun, etc, that would stand between me and
      my success.

3.   Lord, let your power fill all my vessels.

4.   God, give me power over friends and enemies alike, let them
      not be used against me in battle, in Jesus' name.

5.   Lord, empower me over principalities and powers that when
      ever they mention my name, let them be at a great loss.

6.   Lord, use every power that you have in Heaven and in Earth
      to empower me from the top of my head to the soles of my
      feet, against the arrows of enemies.

7.   Lord, I want you to make me a head over all living and non-
      living things, in Jesus' mighty name.

8.   Thank you Lord for all answered prayers.

<u>SCRIPTURE READING</u>: *Psalm 36:1-12*

Memory Verse: "The righteous cry, and the LORD heareth, and deliver-eth them out of all their troubles. The LORD is nigh unto them that are of a broken heart; and saveth such as be of a contrite spirit." Psalms 34: 17 - 18

PRAYER POINTS:

1. Jesus, I welcome you to every loose knot in my life. Come and tighten every loose knot and make every crooked road straight. Bring light to my darkness: God justify and vindi -cate me.

2. The curse of my forefather waging war against God's timing in my life be destroyed by the blood of Jesus.

3. Lord, all the powers that do not want me to get to the top, including agents of darkness talking negatively, waging war against me; bring them down and keep them in a dungeon, in Jesus' mighty name.

4. God, give me power over my future. Straighten my crooked tomorrow and turn my weeping into joy.

5. Lord, deliver me from lack, in Jesus' name.

6. Lord, whosoever and whatsoever is responsible for serious mockery against me and my God, show your power over them; let them be confounded, in Jesus' name.

7. Lord, send inter-continental missiles to demonic monitoring screens watching me; destroy them utterly, in Jesus' name.

8.   CALL THE NAME OF JESUS SEVEN TIMES, and say Lord, loose all that the devil is holding in prison for my life. Every thing that is chained set free and return them to me, in Jesus' mighty name.

9.   Thank you Lord for all answered prayers.

<u>SCRIPTURE READING</u>: *Psalm 23: 1-End*

Memory Verse: *"The Lord is my Shepherd; I shall not want."*
Psalm 23: 1

PRAYER POINTS:

CALL THE NAME OF JESUS ONCE, THE POWER OF RESUR-RECTION THREE TIMES AND HIS BLOOD ONCE.

1.   Lord, today let all my success come into my hands. I don't want it tomorrow for you have said; you will give me daily bread. Therefore, every power that is delaying my success till tomorrow, Lord, destroy it. All the negative words that false prophets have said to me, Lord, I destroy them right now, in Jesus' name.

2.   Lord, let all that has decayed in my life resurrect, in Jesus' name.

3.   Lord, I come against the power of traffic jam in my life and any delay tactics.

4.   Lord, I push my life forward; my stagnant success I push for ward, in Jesus' name.

5.   Every power turning my life anti-clockwise, I say Lord, con-sume them with your fire.

6.   Lord, if Jesus died, if He rose again and if He is coming back again; then answer all my prayers with your power, in Jesus' name.

7.   Lord, I don't want to die lame in the Spirit; Lord I don't want to die deaf in the Spirit, I don't want to die blind in the Spirit; Lord I don't want to die dumb in the Spirit. I know that I am empty, fill me. Let this, my life of emptiness end now, in Jesus' name.

8.   Lord, I don't want to die with your visions in my life, there -fore, let me fulfil all, in Jesus' name.

9.   Lord, give me the power that sees beyond the ordinary.

10. Lord, let your eyes be fastened to my life in all things, in Jesus' name.

11. Thank you Lord for all answered prayers.

SCRIPTURE READING: *Colossians 2: 1- 10*

Memory Verse: *"For with God nothing shall be impossible." Luke 1:37*

PRAYER POINTS:

1.   Lord, let me not become a cast away, in Jesus' name.

2.   Lord, give me power over all the arrows of the enemy, in Jesus' mighty name.

3.   Lord, give me the crown of life.

4.   Lord, write my name in the book of life. I don't want to use my strength any more. Give me power, wisdom, mercy, grace and strength to maintain my crown of life. Lord, I don't want to depend upon my own blood, but the blood of Jesus, in Jesus' name.

5.   Lord, give me power to work for you, in Jesus' name.

6.   Lord, give me wisdom to maintain your power, in Jesus' mighty name.

7.   Lord, I need your power for this end time. Give me the power of answered prayers. Anything that I decree, let it be established, in Jesus' name.

8.   God, give me power of sustenance and maintenance of your goodness in my life, in Jesus' name.

9.   Thank you Lord for answered prayers.

<u>SCRIPTURE READING</u>: *Luke 18:1-8*

Memory Verse: *"Give ear to my words, o LORD, consider my meditation. Hearken unto the voice of my cry, my king, and my God: for unto thee will I pray." Psalm 5: 1-2*

PRAYER POINTS:

CALL THE BLOOD OF JESUS TWENTY-ONE TIMES.

1.   Say, "Blood of Jesus, I dip myself into you"

2.   Lord, all your promises that have been delayed through sin, Lord forgive me and bring them to pass in my life, in Jesus' name.

3.   Lord, give power over myself, over my thoughts, intentions, my eyes, walk, eating and sleeping, in Jesus' mighty name.

4.   Lord, compel me to do your will, in Jesus' mighty name.

5.   Every power stopping me from praying Lord, cast it way, in Jesus' name.

6.   Lord, strengthen me in my walk with you.

7.   Lord, I want you to give me the master key that opens and no man can shut, in Jesus' name.

8.   Lord, uproot every seed of failure in my life, for you created me for a purpose, in Jesus' name.

9.   Thank you Lord for all answered prayers.

SCRIPTURE READING: *Psalm 25: 1 - end*

Memory verse: *"What man is he that feareth the LORD? him shall he teach in the way that he shall choose. His soul shall dwell at ease; and his seed shall inherit the earth." Psalm 25: 12- 13*

PRAYER POINTS:

1. God, make me so powerful that no devil on Earth will be able to determine my success.

2. Lord, I just want to see you again. I want to spend the rest of my life with you; with your power, wisdom, glory, free from Lucifer and his agents. Lord, I want Satan to bow down whenever he sees me, in Jesus' name.

3. Lord, give me power over any place, anybody and anything the devil can use against me.

4. Lord, let me move in your power all the days of my life, in Jesus' name.

5. Lord, let every negative expectation of the enemy and of peo -ple concerning my life be thrown into the dustbin, in Jesus' name.

6. Lord, let me be higher than my mates. Force me to become great; force me to become serious, force me to be anointed, in Jesus' name.

7. Thank you Lord for all answered prayers.

<u>SCRIPTURE READING</u>: *Ephesians 6: 1-End*

Memory Verse: *"Finally, my brethren, be strong in the Lord, and in the power of his might." Ephesians 6: 10*

PRAYER POINTS:

1. Lord, whosoever is in charge of my problem in life, trample them down, in Jesus' name.

2. Lord, any power, any principality that will not allow your word to prosper for good in my life, Lord put them in a dun -geon.

3. Let, every covenant I have made with the devil in the dream through food, and sex, be broken. Lord, break all; covenants with ancestral husband/wife; familiar husband/wife; spiri -tual husband/wife, in Jesus' name.

4. Lord, curse my curses. Let all my blessings be blessed.

5. Lord, I want to enlarge my coast. I am prepared to go foward, I do not want to go backward, in Jesus' name.

6. Lord, give me power over any place, anybody and anything the devil can use against me, in Jesus' name.

7. Lord, give me fingers that succeed, in Jesus' mighty name.

8. Thank you Lord, for all answered prayers.

<u>**SCRIPTURE READING:**</u> *Deuteronomy 28: 1-13*

Memory Verse: "But my God shall supply all your need according to his riches in glory by Christ Jesus." Philippians 4: 19

PRAYER POINTS:

1. Say, "All the gates shut in my life, I command you to open, in Jesus' mighty name".

2. Lord, I want your kingdom to come in my life, in Jesus' name.

3. Lord, I do not want to be an ant in the sight of my enemies, therefore, give me spiritually gigantic figure in the spirit. I do not want to be small in the eyes of my enemies any more.

4. Give me the power of attorney, in Jesus' name.

5. Lord, remove all the spiritual teeth of my enemies as they bark, do not allow them to bite me, in Jesus' name.

6. Lord, keep all the devils together and put them in a dungeon. All the contractual witches, false prophets – let them lose their jobs, in Jesus' mighty name.

7. Any power that is present in my body shadow, working negative forces against me, I command you to leave my body, in Jesus' name.

8. My life has been stagnant; I push it forward, in Jesus' name.

9. God, let your purpose in my life be actualised, in Jesus' name.

10.   Lord, remould me into what you want me to be.

11.   Thank you Lord, for all the answered prayers.

<u>SCRIPTURE READING</u>: *Psalm 24: 1-End*

Memory Verse:*" Save thy people, and bless thine inheritance: feed them also, and lift them up for ever." Psalm 28: 9*

PRAYER POINTS:

1.   Lord, make me somebody in you, in Jesus' mighty name.

2.   Lord, make an everlasting glory, in Jesus' name.

3.   Lord, shine forth your light on every cloudy and dark area in my life, in Jesus' name.

4.   Lord, give me favour with God and men.

5.   Lord, use me mightily for your glory and let all the enemies who wish my downfall be put to shame from head to toe, in Jesus' name.

6.   Lord, remove every spirit of uncertainty from my life and compel me to love you, in Jesus' name.

7.   Lord, all these three jobs - stealing, killing and destroying - that the devil wants to accomplish in my life, let them not be perpetrated whilst I am alive, in Jesus' name.

8.   Lord, let me be higher than my mates. Force me to become great, force me to become serious, force me to become anointed, in Jesus' name.

9.   Thank you Lord, for all answered prayers.

SCRIPTURE READING: *Isaiah 49: 1- End*

Memory Verse: *"Listen O isles, unto me, and hearken, ye people, from far, The Lord hath called me from the womb; from the bowels of my mother he hath made mention of my name. And he hath made my mouth like a sharp sword; in the shadow of his hand hath He hid me, and made me a polished shaft; in his quiver he hid me." Isaiah 49: 1 - 2*

PRAYER POINTS:

CALL THE BLOOD OF JESUS 21 TIMES.

1. Lord, give me a new tongue that the heavens honour. Give me a tongue that the gates of hell shall not stand against, in Jesus' name.

2. Lord, empower me over destiny changers: empower me also over people who send me compliments and praises through gifts that may do more harm than good, in Jesus' name.

3. Lord, empower me over tactical enemies, and over those who parade themselves as friends, in Jesus' name.

4. Lord, give me power against the will and wishes of my ene -mies, in Jesus' name.

5. Lord, empower me over Lucifer himself.

6. Lord, do not let the devil use me against the ministry of Jesus on Earth, in Jesus' name.

7. Thank you Lord, for all answered prayers.

SCRIPTURE READING: *Psalms 91: 1-End*

Memory Verse: *"But, ye shall be named the Priests of the Lord: men shall call you the Ministers of our God; ye shall eat the riches of the Gentiles, and in their glory shall ye boast yourselves." Isaiah 61:6*

PRAYER POINTS:

1. Lord, all those who are in charge of my success – give me power over them, in Jesus' name.

2. Lord, if my pocket, friends, marriage and enemies have con -demned me in any way, come and vindicate me, in Jesus' mighty name.

3. Lord, remove every 'but' in my life. Every "but" in my look, personality, body, account, speech, marriage and all my be -ing – erase completely, in Jesus' name.

4. Lord, I command all giants to GO, in Jesus' mighty name.

5. Thank you Lord, for all answered prayers.

<u>**SCRIPTURE READING**</u>: *Matthew 11: 28-30*

Memory Verse: *"O Lord, I have heard thy speech, and was afraid: O Lord, revive thy work in the midst of the years, in the midst of the years make known, in wrath remember mercy" Habakkuk 3:2*

PRAYER POINTS:

1. Lord, all the evil things that have been done to my inner be -ing, reverse them, in Jesus' name.

2. Lord, take care of every hair on my head; I do not want this head to end up in the hands of herbalists, in Jesus' name.

3. Lord, all demonic powers struggling with my life, powers from my mother's and father's side who have joined together to fight me, Lord help me because I am all by myself. For without your presence in my life they will be victorious over me. Lord, come and fight for me so that I can overcome, in Jesus' name.

4. God, come and immunise my body, soul and spirit, against hell fire, against power and principalities, against Satan, against the bottomless pit, in Jesus' name.

5. Thank you Lord, for all answered prayers.

SCRIPTURE READING: *Isaiah 6:1-9*

Memory Verse:*" In the year that King Uzziah died I saw also the Lord sitting upon a throne, high and lifted up, and his train filled the temple. Above it stood the seraphims: each one had six wings; with twain he covered his face, and with twain he covered his feet, and with twain he did fly. And one cried unto another, and said Holy, holy, holy, is the Lord of hosts: the whole earth is full of his glory" Isaiah 6: 1-3*

PRAYER POINTS:

1.   Lord, do not let your glory depart from my life, in Jesus' name.

2.   Lord, any part of my body-organs that is disloyal to you and loyal to demonic powers, deliver me from them – place them in the heavenly places, in Jesus' name.

3.   Shout, **"LORD EMPOWER ME"** (twice) over anyone and anything that the devil can use to destroy me, in Jesus' name.

4.   Lord, do not let me go back to spiritual Egypt; push or pull me to my Canaan, in Jesus' name.

5.   Lord, do not allow me to become a nuisance: let me not be the one that starts well and does not end well; do not allow my life to be like that of Saul the king, in Jesus' name.

6.   Thank you Lord, for all answered prayers.

<u>**SCRIPTURE READING**</u>: *Revelations 22:1-End*

Memory Verse: *"And he showed me a pure river of water of life, clear as crystal, proceeding out of the throne of God and of the Lamb. In the midst of the street of it, and on either side of the river, was there the tree of life, which bare twelve manner of fruits, and yielded her fruit every month: and the leaves of the tree were for the healing of the nations" Revelation 22: 1-2*

PRAYER POINTS:

1. Lord, let me have access to the Throne Room of grace, when ever I call, in Jesus' name.

2. Lord, give me the gifts and the fruits of the Holy Spirit; I will use them for your glory, in Jesus' name.

3. Lord, reinforce the army of the Lord (your angels) around me; give them at all times power over the Prince of Persia, in Jesus' name.

4. Lord, give me your mark of favour; give me the look, speech and aroma of favour, in Jesus' name.

5. Lord, I want to be different, I want to be unique. Make me unique and spectacular any time and in everything, in Jesus' name.

6. Thank you Lord, for all answered prayers.

<u>SCRIPTURE READING</u>: *Psalm 51: 1-End*

Memory Verse: *The sacrifices of God are a broken spirit: a broken and contrite heart, O God, thou wilt not despise"* *Psalm 51:17*

PRAYER POINTS:

1.   Lord, create in me a clean heart and renew a right spirit within me, in Jesus' name.

2.   Lord, stretch forth your hand of power upon me. For you know that my bones are dry, you are the only one that knows if I can live. Lord, use your wisdom and power to help me so that my bones can live again, in Jesus' name.

3.   Lord, take me through the Red Sea; the manna that came from Heaven, feed me with it, in Jesus' name.

4.   Lord, if I drink water that comes from your rock, I will never thirst again. Lord, I want to drink everlasting water, and eat eternal bread, in Jesus' name.

5.   Lord, let all the errors I have made in the past be corrected by your stripes; let the blood of Jesus wash them away, in Jesus' name.

6.   Thank you Lord, for all the answered prayers.

<u>SCRIPTURE READING</u>: *Psalms 92: 1-End*

Memory Verse: *"But my horn shalt thou exalt like the horn of an unicorn: I shall be anointed with fresh oil." Psalm 92: 10*

PRAYER POINTS:

1.   Lord, break every grave and blood covenant in my life, in Jesus' name.

2.   Lord, give me power over the covenant the enemies made against me; and their looks and the words they say and think about me, in Jesus' name.

3.   Lord, all the powers that are pushing me to do wrong things in order to destroy my future, I come against them by the hand that anchors the whole world, in Jesus' name.

4.   Lord, give me power over negative behaviour and evil thoughts that can destroy my life, in Jesus' name.

5.   Thank you Lord, for all answered prayers.

SCRIPTURE READING: *Ezekiel 37: 1-5*

Memory Verse: *"Whoso offereth praise glorifieth me: and to him that ordereth his conversation aright will I shew the salvation of God." Psalm 50:23*

PRAYER POINTS:

1. (To be prayed by night): **BE ON YOUR KNEES AND SPEAK TO THE GROUND**, saying, Lord, let every good thing that is hidden from me be uncovered. In Jesus' name, I speak to you all ye land, lift up your heads, O ye gates, and let the king of glory enter. From today my glory that is buried in the earth, any place upon this continent or wherever it is planted; I command you to resurrect right now, in Jesus' mighty name.

2. Lord, all the raw materials come from the ground; I must never be in want. All animals and fishes are also from the Earth. Lord God, you brought me from the Earth also; give me power over money, give me power over lack, give me power over fire, and water. Lord empower me over all living and non-living things, in Jesus' mighty name.

3. Lord, wherever my blessings are hidden, bring them out be -fore the sunrise, in Jesus' name.

4. **PROPHESY TO THE LAND** and say, No longer should you be my downfall, but my waterfall, in Jesus' name.

5. Thank you Lord for all answered prayers.

SCRIPTURE READING: *Colossians 2: 1- end*

Memory Verse: *"And ye are complete in him, which is the head of all principality and power:" Colossians 2: 10*

PRAYER POINTS:

1.   Lord, anything that the enemies have planted in my life that has not allowed me to rise; all the powers of darkness (witches and wizards), and their works, Lord, combine them together and burn them all, in Jesus' name. Anything planted in my blood, Lord, flush out and destroy it with your fire in Jesus' name.

2.   Lord, all the hands of negative people in my life, remove now, in Jesus' name.

3.   Lord, chain every power that has no other job than to destroy me; let him lose his job in my life, in Jesus' name.

4.   Lord, every power or person that is waiting for me at the top in order to pull me down, pull them down and destroy their works, in Jesus' name.

5.   Thank you Lord for all answered prayers.

<u>**SCRIPTURE READING**</u>: *Mark 16: 16-17*

Memory Verse: *"And Jesus increased in wisdom and stature, and in favour with God and man." Luke 2:52*

PRAYER POINTS:

1.   Lord, come down and manifest your power and love for me, in Jesus' name.

2.   Lord, anywhere my blessing is hiding, let it be released to - day: destroy all those characters, and familiar spirits that ap -pear to bar me from receiving my blessings.

3.   Lord, earmark me as a symbol of miracles, in Jesus' mighty name.

4.   Lord, any man who does not want me to be a king and is an -gry for the breakthrough of my life, Lord, go now and do justice, in Jesus' name.

5.   Lord, come and immunise my body, soul, and spirit against hell fire, against powers and principalities, against Satan, and against the bottomless pit, in Jesus' name.

6.   Thank you Lord, for all answered prayers.

<u>**SCRIPTURE READING**</u>: *Revelation 22: 1 – end.*

Memory Verse: *"And the spirit and the bride say, Come. And let him that heareth say, Come. And let him that is athirst come. And whosoever will, let him take the water of life freely." Revelation 22:17*

PRAYER POINTS:

1.   (Hold your Bible) Lord, let the blood of Jesus erase all my sins, in Jesus' name.

2.   Lord, give me eternal life at all cost (*Matt. 11: 20-24*), in Jesus' name.

3.   Lord, give me your heart and mind to operate in the super -natural, in Jesus' name.

4.   (Place your Bible upon your head) Lord, let the anointing up-on all your promises in your word sink into my life from the   top of   my   head   to   the   sole   of   my   feet,   in   Jesus'   name.

5.   (Place your Bible upon your heart) Lord, let your words abide in my heart always, and destroy anything that will re move them, in Jesus' name.

6.   Lord, I need your presence, in Jesus' name.

7.   Lord, thank you for all answered prayers.

<u>SCRIPTURE READING</u>: *Psalm 3: 1-End*

Memory Verse: *"Salvation belongeth unto the Lord: thy blessing is upon thy people." Psalm 3: 8*

PRAYER POINTS:

1. Lord, uproot whatever the devil has planted in my life from the time of my conception till this moment, in Jesus' name.

2. Lord, give me another set of spiritual sense organs and break every chain hindering me from walking in the spirit, in Jesus' mighty name.

3. Lord, make straight every crooked way and bring light into my darkness, in Jesus' name.

4. God, if they want to use sinner, saints or the wicked against me; destroy all their handiwork. Lord, empower me over the demonic powers, in Jesus' name.

5. Lord, padlock every mouth that speaks evil against me, in Jesus' name.

6. Lord, deafen every ear that is listening to my conversation when I pray. Cripple all evil feet following me, in Jesus' name.

7. Lord, thank you for all answered prayers.

SCRIPTURE READING: *Amos 9: 13- 15*

Memory Verse: *"But upon mount Zion shall be deliverance, and the re shall be holiness, and the house of Jacob shall posses their possessions." Obadiah vs. 17*

PRAYER POINTS

1. Read *Psalm 94:1* **SEVEN TIMES, CALL THE NAME OF JESUS ONCE AND THE BLOOD OF JESUS TWICE** and say, "I send thunder and brimstone to the citadel of Lucifer and his agents, in Jesus' name."

2. Any man who does not want me to be king and is angry at me for the breakthrough, of my life; Lord, go now and do jus -tice, in Jesus' name.

3. Lord, anybody standing on the west end of my life response -ble for the traffic jam of my life; sack him/her from their as -signment, in Jesus' name.

4. Lord, anybody that says my vision will not be attained; Lord, let that person and his/her household turn to fiction, in Jesus' name.

5. Lord, every vision destroyer in my life that would not want me to enlarge my coast, deal with him as you dealt with King Herod, in Jesus' name.

6. Lord, thank you for all answered prayers.

SCIPTURE READING: Psalm 17: 1- end

Memory Verse: *"As for me, I will behold thy face in righteousness: I shall be satisfied, when I wake, with thy likeness." Psalm 17: 15*

PRAYER POINTS:

1. Lord, if I'm carrying another man's brain or another man's success which is making me unproductive, uproot it and re store my own brain, in Jesus' name.

2. Lord, reschedule my program of success, in Jesus' name.

3. Lord, my life is in your hand. Therefore, every slow thing in my life, push it forward, in Jesus' name.

4. Lord, come against every power that has stopped me from moving forward in Jesus' name.

5. Father, bind all my enemies that are pretending to be friends with chains, until I succeed, in Jesus' name.

6. Lord, when the help of men comes to an end, when what they say does not come to pass, then Lord, arise today and restore my blessings sevenfold. Some people say they will not eat or drink until they destroy my life; therefore let them starve to death, in Jesus' name.

7. Lord, all the rags and tatters in my life, even the ones I cannot see (though I think I am well dressed); stretch forth your right hand of righteousness and remove them and cover my nakedness, in Jesus' mighty name.

8. Lord, thank you for all answered prayers.

<u>SCRIPTURE READING</u>: *Psalm 127:1 – end.*

Memory Verse: "*The, young lions do lack, and suffer hunger: but they that seek the Lord shall not want any good thing.*" *Psalm 34: 10*

PRAYER POINTS:

1. Lord, make me what you want me to be, in Jesus' name.

2. Lord, whatever the enemies are holding onto which belongs to me, restore them all, in Jesus' name.

3. Lord, whatever it will take you, don't let my life bring sorrow to you. Don't let Heaven be disappointed for my sake, in Jesus' name.

4. Lord, don't let me do anything that will bring shame to your name as long as I live, in Jesus' name.

5. Lord, put your mark of favour upon me, and on every facet of my life that the enemy cannot erase, in Jesus' name.

6. Lord, change my life today, for it is senseless to work so hard from early morning until late at night fearing that I will starve to death (*Psalm 127:2*).

7. Lord, thank you for all answered prayers.

TIM OMOTOSO

PRAYER BONANZA
- PART 2 -

"Elias was a man subject to like passions as we are, and he prayed earnestly that it might not rain: and it rained not on the earth by the space of three years and six month." James 5:17

The world we live in is a danger zone. If one is sick, one needs to take medicine as prescribed by a doctor to be cured and if ones does not use the required dose, one is not going to be cured. But unlike medicine, prayer has no overdose but can have an underdose. In *Luke 18:1,* Jesus said *"......that men always ought to pray and not to faint;"*that is the prescribed prayer dose. It is a tablet that should be taken always. If a judge who feared neither God nor man was able to answer the prayer of a widow, how much more God Almighty? (*Luke 18: 2– 8*).

The brand or dose of prayer is day and night; the mode is fervently, or with intense emotion and extremely hot. The reason we are short-sighted and shallow-minded is because we do not pray. Prayer opens up our mind.

Spoken words are important but they have to come from the written word. Jesus said in Matt. 4:4 *"But he answered and said, It is written,* **Man shall not live** *by* **bread** *alone, but by every word that proceedeth out of the mouth of God."* We live not by food/bread BUT by **every word**. So when you are praying you have to back it up with scriptures. Prayers such as "The word of God says *'But my God shall supply all your need according to his riches in glory by Christ Jesus'* Phil. 4:19, therefore I refuse to be poor. I rebuke poverty in Jesus' name."

"Likewise reckon ye also yourselves to be dead indeed unto sin, but alive unto God through Jesus Christ our Lord. Let not sin therefore reign in your mortal body, that ye should obey it in the lusts thereof. Neither yield ye your members as instruments of unrighteouness unto sin: but yield yourselves unto God, as those that are alive from the dead, and your members as instruments of righteousness unto God. For sin shall not have dominion over you: for ye are not under the law, but under grace." Romans 6:11-14

Should you forget the man who died for our sins and refuse to serve him?

Prayer Point: My God wash me with your blood, wash me out of my sin so that I may be clean; let me hear the sound of joy and happiness, wash me Jesus out of sin. Lord, wash me with your blood that the guilt of sin will cease in my life in Jesus' name.

Prayer Point: Lord Jesus, where is your face; deliver me from sin s that are preventing me from seeing you. The sin I inherited from my parents, who also inherited it from their parents, who inherited it from someone else and this can be traced to Adam, making us all sinners. That sin does not allow me to see your face but I want to see your face and the power of your resurrection. I want to look for a manger, God of the angels, God of the Cherubims and Seraphims, God of the Jews, God of the Hebrews, God that put David on the throne even when he was a nobody - in the same manner you that are nobody today will soon become king. My God I want to see you, I don't want to see them. My God, let me see your face, in Jesus' name.

"Hear, O Lord, when I cry with my voice: have mercy also upon me, and answer me." Psalm 27:7

The Bible says draw nigh unto God and he will draw nigh unto you. You need to ask God to visit you with his mercy. If one obtains mercy, people around you will think you are skilled but the truth is that you simply obtained mercy, not that you are so skilled or knowledgeable.

Tell the Lord Jesus that you need his mercy: mercy when I go to school, mercy when I engage in business, mercy when I sleep, mercy when I wake up, mercy when I have food to eat, mercy when I do not have food to eat, mercy when I have money, mercy when I have no money, mercy when I am clothed, mercy when I find myself naked, mercy when I go out, mercy when I come back in, mercy when people love me, mercy when people hate me, mercy when am walking alone, mercy when I am walking with a crowd, mercy outside and inside, mercy when I am alive and mercy when I die.

Prayer Point: Lord, I confess my sins because I am a sinner saved by grace, have mercy on me, forgive me. Do not allow sin to punish me any more. My God, wash me with your blood; let the guilt of sin be removed from me, in Jesus' name.

The Lord has to write your name in the Lamb's book of life. If your name is written in the book of the Lamb, it will be sealed with the blood of Jesus. The blood of Jesus cannot be erased because it is an incorruptible blood. It is not about your righteousness because in your own righteousness you fall short and fail. In praying, you fail, in doing God's will you fail, so you need to depend on the mercy of God.

Prayer Point: Lord my God, your mercy reaches into the heavens, visit me with your mercy, write my name in the lamb's book of life with all your power – My God it doesn't cost you anything to do it, show me your mercy and write my name in the lamb's book of life. I want to enter paradise, I want to wear the crown of life in Jesus' name.

Prayer Point: "My God, you sent Jesus to the Earth, today use your power to write my name in the book of life." Lift up your voice, open your mouth wide and pray, in Jesus' name.

"Submit yourselves therefore to God. Resist the devil, and he will flee from you." James 4:7

Give your body to God, give your mind to God and he will re-mould you and repaint you to make you into what you never imagined you could become.

Prayer Point: Hold your Bible and call the name of Jesus seven times and his blood seven times, "every power of darkness, every unseen power, every power of the devil, I command you in the name of Jesus to get out. Every power that is monitoring every movement of mine today let your eyes be blind. Powers of darkness you will not see me again, the Lord God of Mount Sinai will inflict you with blindness in Jesus' name."

The Bible says "........*resist the devil and he will flee from you*" that is the written word of God (*James 4:7b*).

A cooker is not afraid of fire but can you put your hand into that fire? No, because your hand is not designed for fire but a cooker is designed for fire. That is the kind of prayer you need to pray now. Ask God to design you to hear his voice. Once God designs you to hear his voice you will not misbehave or take a wrong path. When people speak against you, you hear every word because that is the way you have been designed; your flesh is designed to hear when men speak against you but it is not designed to hear from God. You hear when men speak against you and you become vexed. However, when you hear the word of God you are unable to follow it because your flesh is not designed to, but there is a prayer you can pray to remedy this. This is referred to as being re-birthed and becoming born again.

Prayer Point: Lord, re-create me from the crown of my head to the sole of my feet; let your voice take charge of my life, in Jesus' name.

"I beseech you therefore, brethren, by the mercies of God, that ye present your bodies a living sacrifice, holy, acceptable unto God, which is your reasonable service. " Romans 12:1

Giving your body is a reasonable service. If you do not present your body to God you have not even began service. Christ prayed earnestly and the Bible talks about the sweat that came from his body, *"And being in an agony he prayed more earnestly: and his sweat was as it were great drops of blood falling down to the ground."* Luke 22:44

Prayer Point: Lord I give my body, my soul and my spirit back to you; do with me as you will, in Jesus' name.

Prayer Point: According to *Romans 12:1*, Lord I give my body to you, no part of it is for the devil, no part is for sickness, and none of them is for sudden death, in Jesus' name.

Prayer Point: Devil loosen your grip on this body; loosen your grip on my liver, loosen your grip over my kidney. It is written that my body is the temple of the Holy Ghost. Lord I give my body to you in Jesus' name.

Prayer Point: Hold your ears and pray, "Lord I chastise my body and die daily for this cause. These ears to date have been stubborn." The Bible says *"He that hath an **ear**, let **him** hear what the Spirit saith unto the churches; To **him** that overcometh will I give to eat of the hidden manna, and will give **him** a white stone, and in the stone a new name written, which no man knoweth saving he that receiveth it."* Revelation 2:17. You cannot overcome unless you have ears. When you have ears the Holy Ghost tells you how and what to do. **Hold your**

ears, and say "I am tired of doing my own thing, I want my ears to yield dividends, I put my ears into God's archives, Lord refine them for me. I am tired of hearing strange voices, the anthem of sickness, the trumpet and organ sound of infirmities, I command my ears to open only heavenly things in Jesus' name."

These prayers are the mysteries of the kingdom which you have been given to know.

Prayer Point: Lord, I am raising up this leg against amputation. **Raise one leg from your knee and alternate.** Devil, leave my body, my legs are a representative of my body; Lord I give you my leg, my body, accident-free, amputation-free. The Bible *says, "And I will give unto thee the keys of the kingdom of heaven: and whatsoever thou shalt **bind** on **earth** shall be bound in heaven: and whatsoever thou shalt loose on **earth** shall be loosed in heaven." Matthew 16:19*

Prayer Point: Make me your friend, Lord Jesus, don't let me struggle to make paradise **(pray it on your knees or sitting)**.

Prayer Point: Lord I am insuring every part of my body in you, I don't want to be blind, I don't want to be deaf, I don't want to be crippled. As you did to Moses so that he was not feeble, do to me, let me live long in you, in Jesus' name.

Prayer Point: Lord, while I am still alive; lengthen my days in Jesus' name. There is a Herodic demon killing children; the spirit of King Herod, get out of my system, out of family, sudden death get out of my family. From today I separate from them in Jesus' name. The spirit of long life, Lord that is what I want now, Lord add to my years. Every sickness in my body, that is sent to shorten (destroy) my life I send it back to the owner in Jesus' name.

"But when it pleased God, who separated me from my mother's womb, and called me by his grace, To reveal his Son in me, that I might preach him among the heathen; immediately I conferred not with flesh and blood" Galatians 1:15-16

I want you to rebuild your background. The Bible says in *Jeremiah 48:11, "Moab hath been at ease from his youth, and he hath settled on his lees, and hath not been emptied from vessel to vessel, neither hath he gone into captivity: therefore his taste remained in him, and his scent is not changed"-* that Moab had not been emptied from vessel to vessel. Anyone that is already full before coming to Jesus cannot be full of the Holy Ghost. Because you are too full, all the words of God that you hear cannot enter your heart. All those that came to Jesus emptied themselves first and even the woman with the Alabaster oil emptied the entire jar as a symbol of emptying herself, and only then did Jesus have mercy on her.

Some people are like Moab; they have been at ease from their youth and never been emptied from vessel to vessel. You have settled on complacency, saying to yourself: I can never change. You excuse yourself by saying this is how you are forgetting that the Bible says except you repent you shall likewise perish. Before you can go to the next level you have to be emptied from vessel to vessel, your wine must finish before you come to Jesus. If you are too full how can you be refilled? You have to be emptied to be filled; otherwise there is no place (space) to occupy.

Prayer Point: My God I need your mercy, I want to empty myself, fill me Lord in Jesus' name.

Wait and stop running helter-skelter. The inability to wait is a sickness. We are too much in a hurry and not diligent enough to wait for God. You are in the palm of God's hands so just wait. All of you that have dropped off the palm of his hands, **pray this prayer**: "Lord return me into the palm of your hands. The wind of this world has blown me out of your hands." **Close your eyes, call Jesus once and pray**, "Lord, return me into the palm of your hands in Jesus' name."

If you are in God's hands, all your mistakes will be in his hands, all your successes will be in his hands, therefore you will be guiltless. Such people are referred to in the book of Psalms, *"Blessed is he whose transgression is forgiven, whose sin is covered. Blessed is the man unto whom the Lord imputeth not iniquity, and in whose spirit there is no guile." Psalm 32:1-2.* You will be blameless because you are covered by him and are in God's hands; therefore anyone that blames you is blaming the hand of God.

The Bible says in *Proverbs 3:5-6, "Trust in the Lord with all thine heart; and lean not unto thine own understanding. In all thy ways acknowledge him, and he shall direct thy paths."* If you are in His hands you will acknowledge Him, so the very thoughts you have and what you will to do, will come to pass because all you do and think is in his hands, as you recognise that **without him you can do nothing.**

Prayer Point: Lord, I have lost it - I have fallen off the palm of your hand, that is why I am looking for what is NOT lost. Have mercy on me and let me return to the palm of your hand in Jesus' name.

Prayer Point: 'My Lord because I am no longer in your hands, friends say am guilty, my pocket says I am guilty, The account I own finds me guilty, my wardrobe says am guilty, even the sickness in my body says I am guilty, that is why Paul said in *Romans 7: 24* *"O wretched man that I am!* **who shall deliver me** *from the body of this death?"*

Prayer Point: My God, everything around me says I am guilty, my God vindicate me and frighten my friends and enemies alike, frighten my pocket. God frightens the pocket when he opens the windows of Heaven and there is no room to contain your blessing as promised in *Malachi 3: 10* - *"Bring ye all the tithes into the storehouse, that there may be meat in mine house, and prove me now herewith, saith the LORD of hosts, if I will not open you the windows of heaven, and pour you out a blessing, that there shall not be room enough to receive it."*

Prayer Point: Call the blood of Jesus very long, Lord, my pocket says I am guilty and my family are mocking me, asking where my God is. Lord before this year ends surprise them and vindicate me, enough is enough. Lord don't vindicate me if Jesus did not rise from the dead. Don't vindicate me if Jesus was not nailed to the cross, don't vindicate me if Jesus is not coming back again, BUT if all these things are sure to happen then Lord vindicate me in Jesus' mighty name.

"It is the spirit that quickeneth; the flesh profiteth nothing: the words that I speak unto you, they are spirit, and they are life." John 6:63

The word of God is the breath of God. Anyone that has the word of God living in him has the breath of God living in him or her. The devil targets the word of God in one's life; he looks to steal the word of God from you. The word of men brings sickness and a decrease.

Those who have the word of God dwelling in them, healing dwells in them because it is the breath of God, Blessing follows anyone with God's word on the inside of him or her. When God said let there be light, it was not just a saying but it was the breath of God. The scripture says God is light, *"This then is the message which we have heard of him, and declare unto you, that God is light, and in him is no darkness at all." 1 John 1:5.* In effect God simply breathed himself out through the word, because light (God) already existed and whatever exists cannot re-exist because it already is.

Prayer by Tim Omotoso: In the name of Jesus Christ, the son of Mary, the son of the carpenter, I command the windows of Heaven to open. All of you who have grown weary because the journey is long; I command the breath of God to enter into you in Jesus' name, Amen.

"Abide in me, and I in you. As the branch cannot bear fruit of itself, except it abide in the vine; no more can ye, except ye abide in me. I am the vine, ye are the branches. He that abideth in me, and I in him, the same bringeth forth much fruit: for without me ye can do nothing... If ye abide in me, and my words abide in you, ye shall ask what ye will, and it shall be done unto you." John 15:4-5 & 7.

When you abide in Jesus and he abides in you, you will be delivered from every war in your life.

Prayer Point: Lord Jesus I want to abide in you, abide in me. **Call the name of Jesus once and pray loud.**

Prayer Point: Lord, I want to be in you. If I can be in you I know I will be set free in Jesus' name.

Prayer Point: Lord, I want to enter a contract with You. As I seek your face, give me power and mercy to attain the Crown of Life **in** Jesus' name.

"The secret things belong unto the LORD our God: but those things which are revealed belong unto us and to our children for ever; that we may do all the words of this law." Deuteronomy 29:29

SECRETS

God of all secrets, reveal to me the secret of my life as I want to be elevated, enough is enough. Lord the devil is, making me suffer, poverty is making me suffer, my flesh is making me suffer; reveal the secret of my life. If you take this prayer with all your thoughts, with all your body, all your might, all your strength it will be answered.

Prayer Point: Call the name of Jesus three times very powerfully and say, 'My God where is the secret of my life? where is it written? where is my file hidden? who has hidden my file? In whose wardrobe is it? Is it in my mother or father's cupboard? Where is the secret of my life? Lord Jesus I am blind, open my eyes, I want to know what is left for me, where should I go, which way should I take? Lord Jesus, open my eyes - **PRAY.**

Prayer Point: 'Lord that created the stars and named each one, God that created the ants and knows the name of each one, God that created the sands and named them, God of the small rivers, God of the mighty ocean, God that created big and small animals, God that created the lion, God of the sun and moon, God of the wind, God of all secrets where is the secret of my life?' This is how to pray as you prayer language has to be very deep and not shallow.

Prayer Point: Lord what is the secret behind my inability to own a house, buy a car, or pass my exam? I study for exams but I fail.

Who and what is the secret behind these? Reveal it to me Lord as I want to retake the exam.

Prayer Point: Lord of all mysteries, save me from my flesh, give me power over my flesh, I do not want to end up in hell. Give me power to overcome in Jesus' name.

God of all mysteries show yourself, reveal yourself in Jesus' name, Lord my flesh is punishing me as it does not allow me to serve you. My blood is not allowing me to serve you, change the blood I inherited from my father and my mother so that I can serve you in Jesus' name. I am waging war against my flesh today because they are not allowing me to serve you and want to send me to hell BUT I don't want them to send me to hell fire.

Prayer Point: Lord God of all secrets, Lord of all Mysteries, I want you to show me the secret of my life because I want to get to the top. Lord I am suffering, the devil is making me suffer, poverty is making me suffer, my flesh is making me suffer. If you take this prayer point with all your thoughts, all your might, all your strength, it will be answered, in Jesus' name.

"But of the fruit of the tree which is in the midst of the garden, God hath said, Ye shall not eat of it, neither shall ye touch it, lest ye die." Genesis 3:3

What is referred to as the fruit? David said: *"......and in sin did my mother conceive me." Psalm 51:5.* You were born in sin, not that when you came into the Earth you started sinning you were born that way. What is referred to as being born is that you vomit the fruit you ate. Otherwise the Bible would not say: *"......... The dog is turned to his own vomit again;........" (2 Peter 2:22).* You have read this before, it is just that you did not understand it. There are some foods in your system that are working against you. Even when you came into the Earth you were eating in the dream, it is just that you say it does not matter and saying that is the spirit of the devil.

If Judas had vomited that food he would not have not betrayed Jesus. The Bible says in *John 13:27 "And after the sop, **Satan entered** into **him**. Then Jesus said unto **him**, That thou doest, do quickly."* As soon as Judas ate Satan entered into him, but, if he had thrown up that food, he would have thrown up the devil also. Iscariot did not want to betray Jesus but food caused it. Esau did not want to sell his birth right but food was the cause (*Genesis 25:30 -34*). If that spirit enters into one, one will begin to misbehave. On the day King Herod was celebrating his birthday, they were all eating and after Herod ate he began to speak nonsense and the Angel smote him to death and worms began to come out of his body.

If you read *John 6:27-35*, you find Jesus referring to the food of life and he says *"I am the bread of life."* What about the bread of death? Where is that? He spoke about it, but you just did not hear it. Jesus said your forefathers ate manna in the wilderness and they died, yet it came from Heaven. The fruit that killed us in the garden came from Heaven. In *Isaiah 45: 7*, God says *"I form the light, and create darkness: I make peace, and create evil: I the Lord do all these things.*

When you say "Lord, show yourself to me." Which way is he going to reveal himself to you? My people are destroyed for lack of knowledge. Judgement will begin from the house of God. **Call Jesus 3 times very short, then his Blood very long., and say** "Enter into me." When you call the blood and make it very long it will reach down into the foundation of your life and it will begin to push those things out. The secret of the Lord is with them that fear him and he will make them to know his covenant.

Do you understand the name you bear? Jabez could have died in poverty, but he had an understanding of the name. Jacob could have died in his poverty but God showed him that that name was not a proper name. God was with him but not for him, until they wrestled; Jacob took it by force.

Prayer Point: Everything that is hidden in my life through food, Everything I have eaten in the Garden of Eden that is making me suffer, Lord use your Blood to push it out, in Jesus' name.

Prayer Point: Call the Name of Jesus once long and his Blood once: "Everything that I have eaten without my knowledge. Lord, help me. Every food that I have eaten in the midst of the garden, that has made my behaviour very unlike that of God, Lord push it out. Every food that has made me behave like the child of the devil,

Lord, push it out. Jesus, let your death and the power of your resurrection, let it push that food out of my life in Jesus' name."

"Beloved, I wish above all things that thou mayest prosper and be in health, even as thy soul prospereth." 3 John 1: 2

Prayer Point: Lord, I need good health because I know this is indeed a blessing. I need you to repair my kidneys, liver, lungs, heart, etc, in Jesus' name.

Prayer Point: *"And the Lord shall deliver me from every evil work, and will preserve me unto his heavenly kingdom: to whom be glory for ever and ever. Amen."* 2 Timothy 4:18

Lord, I don't want to see evil or have pain for the rest of my life, in Jesus' name.

Prayer Point: *"With long life will I satisfy him, and shew him my salvation."* Psalm 91:16

Lord, if my life is short – lengthen it (after the order of the life of King Hezekiah). Satisfy me with long life, in Jesus' name.

Prayer Point: Lord, the power you used to take money out of a fish, let it come into me in Jesus' name. The power of the Holy Ghost that makes one succeed without struggle, the blessing of God that adds no sorrow, as the Bible says in *Proverbs 10:22 - "The blessing of the LORD, it maketh rich, and he addeth no sorrow with it."* Lord, let the power to succeed, the power of the Holy Ghost, enter into me, in Jesus' name.

Prayer Point: Speak to your life and say "My life, enough is enough of you just staring without moving forward, MOVE NOW. My God, today make a covenant of success with me in Jesus' name.

"Understand therefore this day, that the LORD thy God is he which goeth over before thee; as a consuming fire he shall destroy them, and he shall bring them down before thy face: so shalt thou drive them out, and destroy them quickly, as the LORD hath said unto thee." Deuteronomy 9:3

1. Lord the enemies are shaving off the hair on my head, what happened to Samson; do NOT let it happen to me, in Jesus' name.

2. I want you to pray and say, "Lord you were born for me, not for them. You were born for ME, not for my enemies and that is why they do not believe in you, but I believe in you. Draw a line between me and my enemies, I believe in you but the sickness in my body does not believe in you, I believe in you but the poverty in my life does not, I believe in you but the war of nightmares in my life do not believe in you, I believe in you but the ill thoughts in my mind do not, I believe in you but my weakness does not, and that is the rea -son why I am misbehaving. But today use all your power and might to deliver me from my weakness, in Jesus' name."

3. Lord, all around me people are dying, I do not want to die now; every spirit of death that is pursuing me, let the ground open up and swallow them now, in Jesus' name.

You may have a sickness in your body and death is telling you he is coming for you – tell death, "you can NOT take me, because I am a child of God, (confess this 5 times) in Jesus' name."

1. My God, today, before night falls elevate me (say this twice). All those who have said I will not get to the top – Lord bring them down, in Jesus' name.

2. Everything in my life and every pain in my body that the devil has sent to destroy my life, Lord push it out in Jesus' name. Every power of darkness in my body, in my life, I cast you out in Jesus' name.

3. Spirit of the Prophets, You are the Alpha and the Omega, You are my beginning and my end, You are the consuming fire; every power of darkness that is waging war against me – FIRE OF GOD BEGIN TO DESTROY THEM in Jesus' name.

4. **(Call the name of Jesus very long while seated – as you end it you stand up).** Every messenger of Satan in my body such as sickness, disease, poverty, etc, I command you to get out in Jesus' name.

5. **(Call the Blood of Jesus three times, loud, short and sharp while seated, then call the name of Jesus once very long and stand up as you end it).** Every cancer or any other sick -ness in my body that I am not aware of now which is wait -ing for me in my future, I command you to get out, **(repeat: "I command you to get out" three times – touching every part of your body, bank cards, pictures of loved ones, etc)**, in Jesus' name.

6. Jesus, Son of Mary, cast out of me the spirit that sends one to hell fire, the spirit that causes one to misbehave, the spirit

that is waiting for me on the day of my glory, cast them out of me in Jesus name.

7.   Every spirit of Judas Iscariot in me, Lord, cast it out in Jesus' name.

8.   Lord tear heavens apart for me, in Jesus' name I pray.

"And whatsoever we ask, we receive of him, because we keep his com-mandments, and do those things that are pleasing in his sight."
1 John 3:22

1. If you are the Lord God of the Red Sea, of Mt. Sinai, of Mt. Horeb, then let the ground open and swallow up everyone that is waging war against me. Those speaking against me, saying I will not get to the top and playing with my pocket and account in the powers of darkness, Lord of the Red Sea, Lord of Galilee, where is your face? **Now you will pray and call his name once, his blood once**, "Lord wage war against all those waging war against me in Jesus' name."

2. My God, I have failed you in every way; do not cast me away from your presence and take not your Holy Spirit from me, in Jesus' name.

3. Everywhere the powers of darkness have hidden themselves in my life and everywhere the powers of the kingdom of hell have hidden themselves in my body. Lord cast them out in Jesus' name.

4. Lord, everything I have lost in my life in time past, let it be restored back to me seven fold TODAY! In Jesus' name.

5. Lord, do not let me die like this – do not let me die now. Every good thing a man (woman) can do while alive, let me do it before exiting this Earth.

6. Lord, do not listen to the advice of my enemies, they do not want me to live long - I want to live a long life in JESUS.

7. Lord Jesus Christ, break into pieces the coffin of my death TODAY! The coffin the enemies of my life have manufatured for me, Lord set it on fire NOT tomorrow, NOT next week, NOT next month, NOT next year but **TODAY!!!**

8. The Power of the Holy Ghost enter into me, in Jesus' name.

Whatever is higher than you and you have no power over you is a king. The kings in your life don't allow you to think anymore. Only God knows how many kings reside in your head/thinking faculty - the king of the Philistines, Jebusites, Amalekites, etc, and they are ruling your life. The kings in your life are the strong men that you need to bind and be set free from. You want to pray but you cannot because you are held captive by the strong man. *Matthew 12: 29* says *"Or else how can one enter into a **strong man**'s house, and spoil his goods, except he first bind the **strong man**? And then he will spoil his house."* But instead of binding him, he is binding you.

Prayer Point: Lord set me free from those things and people that are greater than me and have become a king in my life. Lord deliver me from the kings in my life in Jesus' name.

Prayer Point: Call the name of Jesus once and the blood of Jesus once and pray. Strong man of my life, I cast you out in Jesus' name. Get out of my finances, my businesses, my marriage and all that has to with me, in Jesus' name.

Prayer Point: Every garment of shame and garment of iniquity that the enemy has put on me, Lord remove it today in Jesus' name.

There is a garment of iniquity, a filthy garment that the enemy can place on you such as was put on Joshua.

In *Zechariah 3: 3- 5* the Bible says *"Now Joshua was clothed with filthy garments, and stood before the angel. And he answered and spake unto those that stood before him, saying, Take away the filthy garments from him. And unto him he said, Behold, I have caused thine iniquity to pass from thee, and I will clothe thee with change of raiment. And I said, Let them set a fair mitre upon his head. So they set a fair mitre upon his head, and clothed him with garments. And the angel of the LORD stood by."*

Psalm 55: 3 also says: *"Because of the voice of the enemy, because of the oppression of the wicked: for they cast iniquity upon me, and in wrath they hate me."*

Pray this prayer with an understanding and ask the Lord to change your garment today in Jesus' name.

"Now these are the nations which the LORD left, to prove Israel by them, even as many of Israel as had not known all the wars of Canaan; Only that the generations of the children of Israel might know, to teach them war, at the least such as before knew nothing thereof; Namely, five Lords of the Philistines, and all the Canaanites, and the Sidonians, and the Hivites that dwelt in mount Lebanon, from mount Baalhermon unto the entering in of Hamath." Judges 3:1-3

God delivered Israel but left five chiefs/Lords of the Philistines to teach Israel how to war. In our lives we have five chiefs of Philistines which are there to teach us warfare. These five chiefs are namely: 1. Food; 2. Sleep; 3. Sex; 4. Friends; 5. Money. These five chiefs of Philistines fight against our lives.

*"And from the days of John the Baptist until now the kingdom of heaven suffereth violence, and the violent **take** it by **force**." Matthew 11:12*

Now you will pray because there is nothing the chiefs of Philistines cannot take from you; they wait for the day of glory. The five chiefs of Philistines waited for Esau. When they want to wage war against one they want to do a swift work of destruction, and they only need one opportunity. They waited for Esau and they only needed one day to destroy him. "Lord I have tried, I've fasted, I've read your word, I have sang; in fact there's nothing I haven't done but the chiefs of Philistines are still in my life. Today, I know that you left them there to teach me how to war."

It is warfare, if those five chiefs of Philistines are not in your life, you will not be able to hear this type of message and reckon with it; there's nothing they cannot do. They wait for your day of glory then make their move. One of the five chiefs of Philistines, entered into the life of Esau **(Food).** Only one day and they took his glory. The five chiefs of Philistines have existed for a long time, they were in the Garden of Eden and they approached Eve saying: "That **food** is good, you are not serious, eat and enjoy your life." But they did not enjoy life; instead death came in, that is the work of the chiefs of Philistines. They entered into the life of Samson, encouraging him to be intimate with Delilah. In Samson's case two chiefs worked together - **sex and sleep**. The love of **money** destroyed Judas Iscariot.

In fact the five chiefs of Philistines walk together. They say you are my friend (and start that way), eat with me; and then after some time you will sleep together and everything will begin to work together. You will have business dealings together and begin to make money, then the five chiefs will begin to work together; that is why we have five sense organs to teach us how to war. These are the things that are blocking your life's journey. Some of you have been thinking of businesses but have not obtained the business because the five chiefs of Philistines have destroyed it.

These five chiefs of Philistines, follow one about. When you're sleeping, they are there. When you are having sex with someone, they are there. Even when you're eating, they are the name of the food. As you are praying for money they are around. All the friends you have on Earth, it's just that you do not know their real name, they are Philistines. They don't come ordinarily to your life. Have you sat down to ask yourself: how come I met this friend? You don't have time. That is the work of the chief of Philistines;

they will not allow you to have time to think.

Pray for about five minutes; five Chiefs of Philistines and five minutes of prayer. If you are not serious they will overcome you, this is not a prayer of one minute. **You will call Jesus seven times, and you have to be serious with this prayer. Call Jesus seven times and his blood seven times,** Prayer can push the five Chiefs of Philistines to someone else because you do not need them in your life any more. Without your help, Lord, I cannot overcome them. Jesus said in Revelation 3:21, *"To him that overcometh will I grant to sit with me in my throne, even as I also **overcame**, and am set down with my Father in his throne."* Jesus did not just bear the name Jesus, He also had to fight and he overcame. It is not about grace alone but merit, meritorious fight. Some of you may say you have overcome in the physical things such as sex and food, but in the dream, you are sleeping with people and being fed food in the dream and this is part of your life. You may have overcome in the physical but what about in the dream? You will give account of that also.

The five chiefs of Philistines come in all sorts of ways to destroy one's life, call the name of Jesus seven times, and the blood of Jesus seven times. (Every part of your body must participate in this prayer, because they are living right inside of you. The five chiefs of Philistines don't rent a house; they live in one's body). Jesus did not just come and bear the name Jesus, he fought and he overcame. He fought a meritorious fight.

"That the God of our Lord Jesus Christ, the Father of glory, may give unto you the spirit of wisdom and revelation in the knowledge of him: The eyes of your understanding being enlightened; that ye may know what is the hope of his calling, and what the riches of the glory of his inheritance in the saints, And what is the exceeding greatness of his power to us-ward who believe, according to the working of his mighty power," Ephesians 1:17-19

YOU NEED POWER AND WISDOM
"He hath made the earth by his power, he hath established the world by his wisdom, and hath stretched out the heaven by his understanding." Jeremiah 51:15

To live a meaningful life you need to ask God to give you power and wisdom that no one can contend with, power and wisdom that poverty cannot contend with, power and wisdom that powers of darkness cannot contend with, the power and wisdom that Christ used when he was on Earth to overcome the Pharisees and Sadducees.

Prayer Point: Lord, give me the power and wisdom that you used when you died and rose again. Lord Jesus, son of God, if I don't have it, if you don't give me, it means you did not rise from the dead. But I believe that you rose from the dead, I want you to put the devil to shame in my life today.

Once the power and wisdom of God comes, poverty will disappear, you will have food to eat, you will have a house to live in without struggling or sweating. Do you want it? Ask God for the power and wisdom that Jesus used against the scribes, the Pharisees, that they were unable to challenge him. When Jesus answered them they were dumbfounded and could not contend with his wisdom, that is the power and wisdom I want you to ask God for.

Jesus was asked about payment of tax and Jesus said to Peter to catch a fish and open the mouth to retrieve money to pay tax; that is power. Wisdom was demonstrated when he asked for a coin and asked whose image was on it, thus declaring that men are to give unto Caesar what is Caesar's and unto God what is God's.

Prayer Point: Call the blood of Jesus three times and his blood once, Lord I don't want to be foolish any more, plant in me the power and wisdom that the host of hell cannot contend with, give me power and wisdom to live the rest of my life, in Jesus' name.

Prayer Point: Lord I don't want to spoil your altar any more, I don't want to misbehave before you any more, Lord give me power and wisdom so that I will for ever remain in your hands; power and wisdom to wear the crown of Life, power and wisdom so that I will not deny you, power and wisdom in times like these. The power and wisdom that no one has ever had and will ever have in my family, plant it into me, **call the name of Jesus very long and pray**.

"And all things, whatsoever ye shall ask in prayer, believing, ye shall receive." Matthew 21:22

Prayer Point: Lord, give me software of rapture, software to make the rapture, plant it in my life. Software of long life, software to be blessed, I want to live long in you. Plant in me the software of paradise; **(you will call the name of Jesus once but very long),** give me this software so that the people around me will not know where my success is planted in Jesus' name.

Prayer Point: Lord where is my software? Software is what Jabez asked for in *1 Chronicles 4:9-10, "And Jabez was more honourable than his brethren: and his mother called his name Jabez, saying, Because I bare him with sorrow. And Jabez called on the God of Israel, saying, Oh that thou wouldest bless me indeed, and enlarge my coast, and that thine hand might be with me, and that thou wouldest keep me from evil, that it may not grieve me! And God granted him that which he requested."* He was honourable but poor because he had no software. He prayed *"Oh that thou wouldest bless me indeed"*; the word "indeed" is the software. People are blessed but are they blessed indeed? **Tell God:** "Lord, there is nothing you cannot do; before this year ends give me software in my family, give me software so that whatever I lay my hands on prospers."

Prayer Point: Lord, give me the licence to survive! Plant in my life the licence and software to survive. The licence and software to survive in every accident, in every calamity, in every sickness, in every plane crash, in every tsunami, in every hurricane. *"A thousand shall fall at thy side, and ten thousand at thy right hand; but it shall* *not come nigh thee." Psalm 91:7.*

Lord, place the mark of survival in my life. The software to survive anything and everything, *"Saying, Touch not mine anointed, and do my prophets no harm" (Psalm 105:15),* in Jesus' name.

Tell God, "Lord I am tired of a hard drive in life, what I need is software as I don't want a hard drive for my life anymore." If you have the software of the Holy Ghost, you will have five loaves of bread but will feed 5,000, with 12 baskets left over. The Bible *says* *"For promotion cometh neither from the east, nor from the west, nor from the south. But God is the judge: he putteth down one, and setteth up another." Psalm 75:6-7* this is called "software" and it is manufactured in Heaven only.

A man stole all his life and was finally nailed to the cross but the software to get to paradise was in him. Grace is a "software." Paul was complaining about the thorn in his flesh, saying *"For this thing I besought the Lord thrice, that it might depart from me."* But Jesus replied and said to Paul *"........ My grace is sufficient for thee: for my strength is made perfect in weakness. Most gladly therefore will I rather glory in my infirmities, that the power of Christ may rest upon me" 2 Corinthians 12:8-9.*

The Lord said my grace (software) is enough for you; once you have a software on your computer, people will think you are extremely skilful but not so, the software makes what you do easy. There is software that exists and once installed your system cannot be attacked by a virus.

God blesses one with software. You will tell God that your life has a computer but lacks software; all it has is a hard drive and hard disk, therefore you are struggling. All the good ideas that you have are being used by others because you have no software to make it and develop the ideas. The Bible says in *Zechariah 4:6b*

"........... *Not by **might**, nor by **power**, but by my **spirit**, saith the LORD of hosts."* "My Spirit" is the software.

Jesus said wait in Jerusalem until you receive power from on high, that power is software which produces authority with ease. Once you have divine software you will do things with ease and no struggle (authority with ease). While others are having nightmares, software will make you have good dreams. Jacob did not pray, he even used a stone as his pillow but there was software in the stone and angels were playing around him. Lord I need software of prosperity; I want you to change the course of my family through me. I want you to fix your face on me so that I can prosper more than any of them. Lord, I want my household to see your glory on my life; don't let me be a slave to my mates/colleagues.

Software is where the word of God says in *Psalm 127:1 "Except the LORD build the house, they labour in vain that build it: except the LORD keep the city, the watchman waketh but in vain."* While you sleep the software of God will be working for you.

Psalm 126: 1 - 2 "When the LORD turned again the captivity of Zion, we were like them that dream. Then was our mouth filled with laughter, and our tongue with singing: then said they among the heathen, The LORD hath done great things for them." Ask yourself why the blessing was missing and there was captivity-it is because software was lacking. But God wants to turn again the captivity so that you can stop struggling. When God gives you software to prosper it will seem that you are dreaming. That is when you will realise that it is not your hard work but divine software.

It is written that the angels will lift you up if you dash your foot against a stone (*Psalm 91:12*); that is a high level of software. This means the angels will prepare a lift (elevator) for you so you do not dash your foot against a stone. David said even though I walk through the valley of the shadow of death, I will fear no evil for your *software* is with me (*Psalm 23:4*).

Prayer Point: Lord, give me "software" that will elevate me and help me get to the top. Lord I want the top that I do not deserve. The chariot of fire took Elijah to Heaven but he was not burnt (consumed) because his body had become "software".

Prayer Point: You will pray; Lord, give me "software" to break through. I do not want to suffer before I make it in Jesus' name.

In the world today there is a power ruling it and if you do not make it in the Holy Ghost the powers of darkness will be directing and dictating your life. **You will now ask for the power of the Holy Ghost, the power that moves one's life forward.** The Apostles were fishermen before but when the power of the Holy Ghost entered them Peter won 3,000 souls in a few minutes, and that without a microphone.

Prayer Point: Power of the Holy Spirit, when I am going out, go out with me; when I come in, come in with me; when I wear clothes, be there. Whatever I do, Holy Ghost, be there with me, in Jesus' name.

"For though we walk in the flesh, we do not war after the flesh (for the weapons of our warfare are not carnal, but mighty through God to the pulling down of strongholds). Casting down imaginations, and every high thing that exalteth itself against the knowledge of God, and bringing into captivity ever thought to the obedience of Christ."
2 Corinthians 10:3-5

There are powers created to make people suffer, that is their mission and assignment. It is the reason they exist. You need to wage war on such powers so you can overcome and be set free.

Prayer Point: Call the name of Jesus once very long and loud and say "Every power that has been assigned to punish me, Lord push them out now in Jesus' name."

"And when it was day, certain of the Jews banded together, and b o u n d themselves under a curse, saying that they would neither eat nor drink till they had killed Paul." Acts 23:12. Lord, all those who have taken a vow saying they will NOT eat nor drink until they see my death. Lord, let the ground open up and swallow them in Jesus' name.

Prayer Point: Lord withdraw every plan that the devil has for my life in Jesus' name.

Prayer Point: Holy Ghost fire burn every sickness in my body, burn every debt and problems that I have in Jesus' name.

"And the spirit of the Lord shall rest upon him, the spirit of wisdom and understanding, the spirit of counsel and might, the spirit of knowledge and of the fear of the Lord;" Isaiah 11:2.

Prayer Points:

1. I need the fear of the Lord in my life. Spirit of the fear of the Lord enter into me. Lord, I need your fear in my heart in Jesus' name."

2. Lord, whatsoever is holding my blessing, whosoever is hold -ing my destiny, force him/her to release it.

3. Lord Jesus, by violence before the sun rises let my blessing knock and break my door open.

4. Lord, I do not know who is in charge of the story of sorrow in my life, whether it's my friends or enemies, whoever it is. POWER - the kind Prophet Moses used when they waged war against him and said the ground should open and swal -low his enemies – "that kind" of POWER, let it descend to day on my enemies in Jesus' name.

5. Lord, the spirit that discourages people from helping me, CAST IT OUT IN Jesus' name.

6. Lord, whatever things the Devil has planted in me that he is using to use me against myself, Lord cast them out in Jesus' name.

7. **Call the blood and name of Jesus once very long and loud!** Lord God change my story, change my biography, my past is

bad. Change my story as the story of Jabez was changed. I am tired of the mockery of people. Disgrace my disgrace, trouble my troubles, confuse my confusion, confound my enemies, take my home address from their diary, delete my number from their cell phones/mobile phones – those who are looking for my life, blind them when they are near my house, in Jesus' name.

8. Lord Jesus Christ, wherever my blessings are hiding, let them locate me now in Jesus' name.

"And David smote them from the twilight even unto the evening of the next day: and there escaped not a man of them...And David recovered all that the Amalekites had carried away: and David rescued his two wives. And there was nothing lacking to them, neither small nor great, neither sons nor daughters, neither spoil, nor any thing that they had taken to them: David recovered them all." 1 Samuel 30:17-19

Prayer Points:

1.   Lord, do not let the joy of my life be ruined, in Jesus' name.

2.   Lord, make me a role model in good behaviour, in anoint -ing, in blessing. I want to be a role model in everything good, from both the spirit and the physical. Let all my friends fear you because of me in Jesus' name.

3.   **You are going to send missiles, intercontinental ballistic missiles to the camp of your enemies. Call the blood of Jesus three times and the name three times, soak yourself in the blood of Jesus, soak your children in the blood of Jesus,** Confess and say "I'm free from sudden death, free from sicknesses and infirmity, free from debt, I'm free from powers and principalities; in Jesus' name I pray."

4.   **Face any angle and stretch forth your Bible, cast away devils from your home, cast away Lucifer and demons from your finance, cast out every demon from your life in Jesus' name. Call the name of Jesus once and the blood of Jesus three times and pray.**

5.   **Be on your knees, call the name of Jesus once and the**

blood of Jesus once, Lord restore to me what the devil has stolen and I have lost, I am not supposed to be a beggar; restoration, Lord, in Jesus' name.

6. **Blood of Jesus, the name of Jesus,** the mark of death on me, Lord uproot it, in Jesus' name. "Any tree that you have not planted in my life, uproot Lord in Jesus' name."

7. Lord empower me over the sand and the pebbles, over sea and the land, over water and fire, over whosoever and whatsoever, over negative and positive, empower me over death and life, empower me over the graveyard, empower me over accident, over everybody and anyone, over the wind and over the air. Lord empower me, empower me, give me power over anything and everything. **Call the name of Jesus and then the blood of Jesus once – PRAY!**

8. Jesus moved forward and did not decay in the Sepulchre but He rose from the dead, He is now seated in the heavens. "My life, I command you to move forward," if any part of your body is decaying they should receive life now in Jesus' name.

9. **Pray this prayer in your mother tongue, pray for whatso -ever you desire in Jesus' name.**

10. All the people and things on Earth that is not greater than God must not be mightier than me. **Call the name of Jesus once and the Blood once.**

11. **Call the Blood first before the name of Jesus, (three times**

each.) Let the fire of God go to the camp of all my Philistines and destroy. Let the fire of God go to the camp of all my Amalekites and destroy, spare nothing, spare no one. Those people who say I should not worship my God, those problems, those powers, those principalities, those witches, those wizards, those with occult powers; let the fire of God go to anywhere they may be holding a meeting against me and destroy all in Jesus' name.

12.   "Lord, from this hour let the power that raised Jesus from the dead raise my life up."Lord, the power that raised Jesus from the dead, raise my life up today; no more procrastination. My Lazarus I command you - rise up and come forth; in my business come forth, in my marriage come forth, in my pocket come forth, among my children, come forth in Jesus' name."

Even before you were born you had been raised with Jesus but you never knew because people have placed their hands on your success, if your Lazarus is still in the grave Jesus is risen from the dead, and will raise your Lazarus up.

"For we wrestle not against flesh and blood, but against principalities against powers, against the fullers of the darkness of this world, against the rulers of the darkness of this world, against spiritual wickedness in high places." Ephesians 6:12

Prayer Points:

1. Lord, give me power over anyone that is envious of me. Power over anyone whose mind is against me; Lord, they smile when they see me but their minds are not smiling. Give me power over them, in Jesus' name.

2. Lord, I don't know who is for me; you are the only one that is able to test their minds. Son of the Living God, send brim stone and fire and destroy whosoever or whatsoever is against me. Lord, do not sleep, do not slumber – Fire of the Holy Ghost, go and destroy them in Jesus' name.

3. Lord, whosoever that says that I will not get to the top – bring them down today. Let me hear the shout of the Amale -kites (my enemies) today, not tomorrow, in Jesus' name.

4. Lord, send help for me from above. I am tired of the help of man; when they promise they never fulfil. God of Heaven, open the windows of Heaven to help me. All my enemies that say I will not get to the top, let the ground open and swallow them up. I command the ground to open and swallow them up, in Jesus' name.

5. Lord, anything that is my life that will not allow me to get to Heaven, cast it out, in Jesus' name.

6.   Every spirit that is waiting for me on top; all those spirits that do not see me when I am suffering, but when my life is movi -ng forward they see me. All such spirits that are waiting for me; let the fire of the Holy Spirit begin to burn them, in Jesus' name.

7.   Lord, wherever ALL my enemies are hiding as the lions hide for their prey, Lord send Holy Ghost fire to destroy them in Jesus' name.

8.   Lord, I want to enjoy my life in and with you, but there are people who do not want that for me, they are angry at my testimonies, they are NOT happy at my success. Holy Ghost fire - visit them, in Jesus' name.

9.   Lord God, it's not difficult for you to save the powerful or the powerless, they are both the same to you.(2 Chronicles 14:11) The enemies are powerful, I'm powerless they have might I don't have power. Use your might to save my weak self, in Jesus' name.

10.   Lord, since it is not he that wills but God that shows mercy (Romans 9:16), let your signature be on me. Lord Jesus Christ, son of David (Pray shouting loudly), every spirit of misbehaviour, push it out, cast it out of me, in Jesus' name.

"Wherefore God also hath highly exalted him, and given him a name which is above every name: That at the name of Jesus every knee should bow, of things in heaven, and things in earth, and things under the earth"
Philippians 2:9-10

Prayer Points:

1.   In the name of Jesus, Son of Mary! In the name of Jesus Christ, Son of a carpenter! I command the windows of Heaven to open over me in Jesus' name.

2.   Lord, let prosperity cease to be my enemy, in Jesus' name.

3.   Lord Jesus, empower me over all the strategies and devices of the enemies, in Jesus' name.

4.   Lord, the Star of my Destiny should not be in the sea; it should be in the sky, in Jesus' name.

5.   Lord, I want to make things happen throughout this year, for my family, business, job, and ministry (church), in Jesus' name.

"Behold, I give unto you power to tread on serpents and scorpions and over all the power of the enemy; and nothing shall by any means hurt you." Luke 10:19

Prayer Points:

1. Lord, give me the type of miracle, blessings, success and wealth that cannot be contained by man on earth; great bless -ings that will cause me to be a blessing to others, in Jesus' name.

2. Lord, give me a new tongue that the heavens respect; give me a tongue that supersedes that of my enemies and friends. Let my words be recognised and respected above all others in Jesus' name.

3. Lord, empower me over destiny changers. Empower me over people who send me compliments and praise, when they are actually cursing me, in Jesus' name I pray.

4. Lord, give me power against the will and wishes of my ene -mies, in Jesus' name.

5. Lord, let every day be like Christmas for me, in Jesus' name.

6. Lord, all the clothes I am wearing (in the spiritual realm) which are filthy – spelling my doom; let the Holy Ghost fire burn them to ashes.

7. Lord, curse my curses and let all my blessings be blessed in Jesus' name.

8. Lord, cast out every spirit of uncertainty in my life, in Jesus' name.

9.   Lord, compel me to do good, and compel me to love in Jesus' name.

10. Lord, give me power over my associates; give me power over members of my household, in Jesus' name.

11. Lord, count me among the few that will make it in life, in Jesus' name.

12. Lord, I want to have testimonies throughout this year, I want to tell of your greatness; therefore, anyone that will not allow your vision in me to come to pass, lock them in your dungeon, in Jesus' name.

13. Lord, write off all my spiritual debts; every sin that is capable of stopping me from prospering – write them off in Jesus' name.

14. Lord, all the three jobs of stealing, killing and destroying, which Herod wants to accomplish in my life – let them not be perpetrated while I'm alive, in Jesus' name.

15. Lord, during this year I want to win more souls than anybody in Jesus' name.

16. Lord, remove all the spiritual teeth of my enemies, in Jesus' name.

17. *"And he said, My presence shall go with thee, and I will give thee rest. And he said unto him, If thy presence go not with me, carry us not up hence." Ex. 33:14-15.* Lord, anywhere your glory will not follow me – do not let me go there, in Jesus' name.

18.   Lord, every good thing that you have for people who trust in you, don't let me sweat for it in Jesus' name.

19.   Lord, I go out every day to look for what to eat; don't let any thing eat me up, let me not become a prey to the enemy in Jesus' name.

20.   Lord, give me power to pursue your power all the days of my life, in Jesus' name.

21.   Lord, give me power over my day of weakness in Jesus' name.

22.   Lord, give me power over my familiars, in Jesus' name.

23.   Lord, use whatever power you have in Heaven and Earth to transform my life, in Jesus' name.

24.   Lord, I don't want to be an ant in the sight of my enemies. Give me a spiritually gigantic figure in the spirit that no power can stand before me.

25.   Lord, don't let me die ordinary; give me your power, your love and your wisdom.

26.   Lord, I confess my life as a sinner; have mercy upon me a sin -ner. Lord, I believe in your righteousness in Jesus' name.

27.   Lord, give me the gift you give to anybody who seeks your face early in the morning. Let it be greater than anyone else who seeks you at any other time, in Jesus' name.

Prayer Points:

1.   Lord the enemies have spoken against you in my life and are limiting the Holy One of Israel. I am lifting up my eyes to the hills because that is where my help comes from.

    Recite Psalm 121:
    ¹I will lift up mine eyes unto the hills, from whence cometh my help. ²My help cometh from the LORD, which made heaven and earth. ³He will not suffer thy foot to be moved: he that keepeth thee will not slumber. ⁴Behold, he that keepeth Israel shall neither slum -ber nor sleep. ⁵The LORD is thy keeper: the LORD is thy shade upon thy right hand. ⁶The sun shall not smite thee by day, nor the moon by night. ⁷The LORD shall preserve thee from all evil: he shall preserve thy soul. ⁸The LORD shall preserve thy going out and thy coming in from this time forth, and even for evermore.

2.   Power of limitation I cast you out, I cast out every power that has limited me and limited my success in Jesus' name.

3.   Lift up your Bible and pray "every power of darkness that has limited me from getting to the top, let the ground open and swallow them up in Jesus' name." Lord, lift my head up and change my story from today in Jesus' name.

4.   Father, let my Goliath be destroyed today in Jesus' name.

"My mercy will I keep for him for evermore, and my covenant shall fast with him." Psalm 89:28

Noahdic Covenant - it is the covenant of Noah that can make you escape hell fire through the name of Jesus, just as Noah escaped the flood. God was angry with everyone except Noah. On the day of God's anger, on the day there is natural disaster, flood, fire, etc. "I will escape as Noah escaped in Jesus' name. The covenant you made with Noah, Lord, make it with me in Jesus' name. Spare my life, O Lord."

Abrahamic Covenant - is the one where anyone who curses you is cursed and anyone who blesses you is blessed. "Lord, the covenant you made with Abraham, if it stays and you know that Abraham is your friend indeed, then make that covenant with me in Jesus' name."

Mosaic Covenant - that at 120 years of age Moses' eyes never dimmed and he could not be buried by mere human beings. It is an everlasting covenant, one of durability. "The covenant you made with Moses that you showed your face to him, I want to see your face before I depart this life. I need your presence in my life, let your face shine upon me in Jesus' name. The covenant you made with Moses that death had no victory over him, sickness had no victory over him, make it with me in Jesus' name."

The Spirit of double portion upon Job. – "Lord you turned the captivity of Job, I don't need his sufferings any more, only the blessing of the later days of Job   I need, in Jesus'

name. Lord as you turned the captivity of Job; turn my captivity and return all I have lost in Jesus' name."

Davidic Covenant - Lord I am tapping into the Davidic cove
-nant; the sure mercies of David. Lord drag me into the sure
mercies of David, when others are judged, spare me because
of the covenant of David that I am tapping into today in
Jesus' name.

The favour upon Mary the mother of Christ Jesus is enough
for me. The favour upon Mary let it fall upon me in Jesus'
name, the favour you had that made an angel appear in the
physical; highly favoured among women.

Messianic Covenant – 'All the blessings in the Bible, the
fullness of God the father upon Christ; Christ Jesus I tap into
your covenant. The covenant that states that all power in
Heaven and on Earth belong to you. The New Testament
covenant be upon my life in Jesus' name. Lord I am tapping
into your covenant, the One of *"This is my beloved son in whom
I am well pleased"* in Jesus' name.

Everlasting Covenant - Lord make an everlasting covenant
with me that whatever happens I will not go to hell fire.
Make an everlasting covenant so that I will make Heaven at
all cost, in Jesus' name.

"Behold, the former things are come to pass, and new things do I declare: before they spring forth I tell you of them." Isaiah 42:9

Prayer Points:

1. Lord this year is passing away, I see myself like dry bones and I want flesh to cover my bones, because they are dry bones; but today cover me with flesh, let your breath enter me, if I die like this without your breath then I would have wasted my life. God you created the stars, God of the 24 Elders; God you hid Jonah in the stomach of a whale; Lord, Lord, Lord, Lord, Lord - Do not let my enemies mock me and laugh at me. Dry bones of my life, dry bones of my life, thus saith the Lord, let flesh cover me. Dry bones that do not allow me to pray, to fast, to do your will; I want flesh to cover me in Jesus' name.

    "My times are in thy hand: deliver me from the hand of mine enemies, and from them that persecute me." Ps. 31:15

2. Lord, I give my body, my soul and my spirit back to you; do with me as you will in Jesus' name.

3. **(Shouting very loudly)** Lord, before this year ends vindicate me, vindicate me and surprise me, in Jesus' name.

4. Make me your friend Lord Jesus, don't let me struggle to make paradise **(pray it on your knees or sitting)**

5. Lord in the name of Jesus, do not let the key of my life remain in the hand of man, because if it does they will refuse to open the door to my blessings.

6.   **Pray for the gifts of the Holy Spirit, you need all of them.**
'Holy Spirit **(touch every part of your body)**, fill my body,
touch every part of my body; all the nine gifts of the Holy
Spirit I am inviting you, this body is for you, from my head
to my fingers. Every part of my body - fill it and take over
this body in Jesus' name.'

*"And straightway the father of the child cried out, and said
with tears, Lord, I believe; help thou mine unbelief."*
Mark 9:24

7.   Lord Jesus, Help my unbelief! In Jesus' name.

IT IS YOUR TIME TO MAKE IT IN JESUS' NAME.

ADBN | ANCIENT OF DAYS BROADCASTING NETWORK

GREAT NEWS!
Ancient Of Days Broadcasting Network IS BORN!

TIM OMOTOSO GLOBAL OUTREACH PRESENTS ADBN

*Ancient Of Days Broadcasting Network (**ADBN**) is the TV Media arm of Tim Omotoso Global Outreach, propagating the gospel of Jesus Christ to this generation with signs following. **ADBN** was launched on 1st March, 2013 and it provides Christian broadcast on digital satellite networks distributed through multiple satellite broadcasting platforms. **ADBN** reaches millions of households in Africa, Europe, United States of America, North America, Canada, and Mexico.*

HOW TO TUNE ADBN ON DSTV IN AFRICA

1. *Go to Menu*

2. *Then to Advanced options*

3. *Select Dish installation*

4. *Enter the Password: 9949*

5. *Select the 2nd Network and change it to (DStv IS7) then press enter. (as all the Networks are disabled, apart from the first Home network)*

   Use these settings: Frequency: 12562, Symbol Rate: 26657, FEC: 2/3, Polarization: Horizontal.

6. *Use NIT: Yes*

7. *Accept all display values and leave screen*

8. *Then press EXIT and wait until the Decoder finishes to scan all the Networks. But in some of the Decoder's they will automatically reboot then scan.*

9. *Press TV function on your remote then scroll down to Public IS7, then browse for ADBN.*

Satellite Settings for ADBN

G19 (Satellite for USA, North America, Canada, Mexico)

Frequency: 12.682 GHz
Position: 69 degrees East
Polarization: Horizontal
FEC: 1/2
Symbol rate: 26.657

EF28k (Satellite transponder for Africa, Europe including United Kingdom)

Frequency: 12.562
Position: 68.5 East
Polarization: Horizontal
FEC 2/3
Symbol rate: 26.657

To partner with ADBN in turning the hearts of men back to God:
Contact us on:

Email: info@timomotoso.org **or** jdiadmin@timomotoso.org
Tel: +27 (0) 31 301 9039 | +27 (0) 76 155 4712 | +44 (0) 79 8451 1941

Tim Omotoso has a weekly TV program entitled **JUST AS I AM**, which can be viewed on the following stations:

SOWETO TV on DSTV *channel 251 every Sunday at 07:00 (GMT + 2)*

ONE GOSPEL on DSTV *channel 331 every Friday at 08:30 and 20:30, also on Sunday at 08:30 (GMT + 2)*

INSPIRATION TV on **SKY** *Channel 587 Every Wednesday and Thursdays at 22:00 (GMT). In South Africa Inspiration is available on the TOP TV satellite.*

LESEA BROADCASTING:

Middle East TV (METV) *Every Saturday at 14:30 (GMT + 3) and Sunday at 11:30 (GMT + 3)*

World Harvest TV (WHT) *USA Every Sunday at 19:00 (Eastern Time)*

Also watch "**Just as I am**" services online at:

www.livestream.com/justasiam
www.ustream.tv/channel/jesus-dominion-international

For more information visit: *www.timomotoso.org*
You can contact us by email: *info@timomotoso.org*

CONTACT US:

SOUTH AFRICA: *+27 (0)76 1554712 & +27 (0)31 3019039*
UNITED KINGDOM: *+44 (0)75 36781057 & +44 (0)79 29154214*
NIGERIA: *+234 (0)80 37256222 & +234 (0)803 2243333*
FRANCE: *+ 33 (0) 95 080 7313 & + 33 (0) 65 931 1194*